Adventures of the Souls

Self-Reflections of Selected Souls

Samuel W. Hale, Jr.

WESTBOW
PRESS®
A DIVISION OF THOMAS NELSON
& ZONDERVAN

Copyright © 2016 Samuel W. Hale, Jr.
Interior Illustrations by Jonathan J. Hale, Sr.

All rights reserved. No part of this book may be used or reproduced by any means, graphic, electronic, or mechanical, including photocopying, recording, taping or by any information storage retrieval system without the written permission of the author except in the case of brief quotations embodied in critical articles and reviews.

Scripture taken from the King James Version of the Bible.

WestBow Press books may be ordered through booksellers or by contacting:

WestBow Press
A Division of Thomas Nelson & Zondervan
1663 Liberty Drive
Bloomington, IN 47403
www.westbowpress.com
1 (866) 928-1240

This is a work of fiction. All of the characters, names, incidents, organizations, and dialogue in this novel are either the products of the author's imagination or are used fictitiously.

Because of the dynamic nature of the Internet, any web addresses or links contained in this book may have changed since publication and may no longer be valid. The views expressed in this work are solely those of the author and do not necessarily reflect the views of the publisher, and the publisher hereby disclaims any responsibility for them.

ISBN: 978-1-5127-5321-9 (sc)
ISBN: 978-1-5127-5320-2 (e)

Library of Congress Control Number: 2016913152

Print information available on the last page.

WestBow Press rev. date: 8/31/2016

Contents

Introduction vii
Endorsements ix

Section 1
IN HIS IMAGE

Upon Arrival 1
Overcoming My Constraints 5
Who's There? 7
The Great Escape 9
Know Thyself 11
Feeding Time 15
Learning to Walk 17
Independence Day 19
The Inner Struggle 21
Getting the Help I Need 23

Section 2
SOUL MEN AND SOUL WOMEN

A Special Gift 27
Challenges to Service 29
Listening to the Right Voice 31
Close Encounters 33

In My Right Mind 37
A Second Chance to Live 41

Section 3
RECOMPENSE

Mission Aborted 47
Destined for Damnation 51
An Intermission 55
Souls on Trial 57
Because of Me 61

Introduction

One of the most awesome and sobering statements in the Bible highlights the *soul*: "and man became a living soul."

Biblicists, theologians, psychologists, physicians, poets, lovers, and fools have all made noted explanations, definitions, and references to the *soul*. For whatever reasons, those references to the *soul* always seem to focus on that creature called *man*. Of all the awesome and magnificent things that happened in the creation, of all the awesome and magnificent creatures that God created, only to man was this acclamation and affirmation made,

> And the LORD God formed man of the dust of the ground, and breathed into his nostrils the breath of life:
> and man became a living soul." (Genesis 2:7)

Only to man was there a personal inclusion of the essence of God in the nature of all that which God created.

The biblical terms that refer to the *soul*, identify certain qualities and characteristics that give insight to the awesome essence of a *"soul"*. In the Old Testament, the Hebrew term for soul—*nephesh*—refers to the "life principle" of a human being. It is distinguished from the "body", but is inclusive of it—it was an animated body. It is not the same as the spirit, yet it includes the workings of the spirit. The Hebrew concept of *nephesh* expresses the ideas of the totality of the "living being", the self, the person—physically, emotionally, mentally, and spiritually.

In the New Testament, the Greek term *psuche* is used to express the idea of the "life" of the human being, which is expressed in the body *(soma)* and the flesh *(sarx),* under the power of the spirit *(pneuma).*

Man is a Soul. At the moment of his creation, when the Spirit of the Living God was infused into his being and began animating his earthly essence, man became a Soul – a Living Soul!

The soul is an eternal entity. It is conceived in the Eternal Mind of God – "Before I formed thee in the belly I knew thee …" (Jeremiah 1:5)—and thus it transcends time, space, and matter.

The soul is a gift of God to all creation. All that a soul has is a gift from God. God is truly the Donor of every soul. Job was right: "The Lord gave, and the Lord has taken away; blessed be the name of the Lord" (Job 1:21).

As long as a soul is in the mind of God, it is eternal! Even in death, the soul is still eternal. It exists then either in the presence of God in heaven, or in the absence of God in hell—both of which are eternal.

From the dawn of time, various thoughts, ideas, and expressions have been made about the soul. But what insights might the soul confirm about itself?

This treatise is an effort to shine some light on that very matter. Listen to these accounts of various souls that you may know or may have heard about.

Endorsements

Here is a deep-thinking pastor and author who uses the description of natural fetal and human development to explain faith development and the fulfillment of soul. The approach is unique. The writing is clear. Hang on for an uplifting journey in prose that brings you to an even more heavenly conclusion.

> Pastor W. G. Robinson-McNeese, MD
> New Mission Church of God, Springfield, IL
> emergency medicine physician, Springfield, IL

Adventures of the Souls is an invitation by a man of God for the reader to journey with him into the realms of living souls and the Living God who created them. The writer leads the reader to enter into the realms of the mind, consciousness, and the spirit. Very skillfully, the reader is shown glimpses of God working in the history of humankind for His glory. He ordains various souls to undertake missions within the mission of their Creator God.

It is a great adventure, one that requires a mind freed from the boundaries of just the physical, and one that believes in the Creator God.

Robert F. Newkirk
former chair of deacons
Fifteen Avenue Baptist Church, Nashville, TN
professor of biology (ret.)
Tennessee State University, Nashville, TN

What a magnificent journey of spiritual self-discovery that transcends the human experience beyond personality and characteristics. The author uses first-person illustrations to enhance the trip and allows the traveler to relate with each soul, leaving the reader in awe!

V. Erlena Mims
customized course development
Concepts of Christian Education
Kennedale, TX

Behold, all souls are mine; As the soul of the father, so also the soul of the son: the soul that sinneth, it shall die. (Ezekiel 18:4)

The LORD shall preserve thee from all evil: he shall preserve thy soul. (Psalm 121:7)

Section 1
IN HIS IMAGE

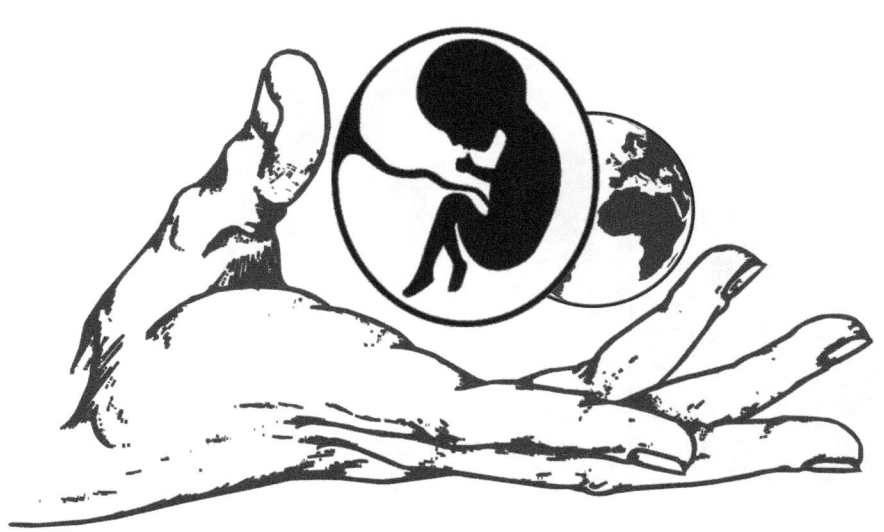

Upon Arrival

Friday the thirteenth was our departure date. Some of us had left the day before, and still others of us were scheduled for future departures. We had no knowledge of our destinations or of how long our stays would be there. Our missions were one and the same—to impact our Hosts and all we encountered in such a way that the image, nature, and will of our Donor would be revealed in them.

The journey, though millions of miles in human measurement, was instantaneous in our Donor's mind. Before we knew it, we were each at our respective destinations. We had experienced a transferal from eternity to what was called Earth, a rotating orb in a solar system of one of the heavenly galaxies called the Milky Way. Unlike our realm of origin, this place existed under the constraints of time, space, and matter. And throughout our stay on Earth, we continued to learn and adjust to those constraints. It was also under these constraints that we had to accomplish our mission.

Our arrivals were called *conceptions*! We immediately began experiencing some of the constraints of existence in the realm of time, space, and matter. Our point of entry was called a *womb*.

Some of us had the same destination, but we were still each our own beings. Not long after our arrivals, we were all given names!

They were usually given at the discretion of our Hosts. There was one of us who had been given a name by our Donor, which his Host gladly and humbly referred to. For the most part, though, it was up to us to give meaning to our names.

Our hosts were all called *females*. They had been so constructed by our Donor to assist in the transitional stage of our entry to our assigned mission. Upon our arrivals, we began to be transformed—developed—into a fleshly matter, or substance, that resembled that of our Hosts. We later discovered that, though our fleshly substance was the same, there were slight differences in certain fleshly elements of our beings. Some of those elements resembled those of our Hosts, while others of those elements resembled those of another being who claimed as much identification with us as our Hosts. They were called *males*.

For a period of time—approximately nine months—we were confined to a space called the *womb* of our Hosts. While in those wombs, our fleshly elements grew larger. We developed hearts and lungs and arms and legs and feet and mouths and tongues; we developed digestive systems, brains and nervous systems, and other systems needed for us to function efficiently and effectively on our own in our new environment.

Certain of our *Donor qualities* also began to adapt to and develop with our fleshly components, in order for us to be able to fulfill our mission responsibilities.

One of those Donor qualities is *consciousness*! With consciousness, we are aware of our feelings, emotions, thoughts, and actions. Consciousness also allows us to experience the power and presence of our Donor within us.

Another Donor quality is *conscience*! Conscience is that element of the soul that monitors and regulates the soul's compliance with the holiness of God.

With conscience, we are always in contact with the mind of our Donor. With conscience, we would always be able to know and understand His purpose and will for us at every moment in our earthly existence.

With conscience I am able to monitor and regulate my own compliance with the holiness of God. I don't ever want to experience what is called a "seared conscience." I don't ever want to operate in total resistance of and defiance to the holiness of my Donor.

Conscience allows the mind of our Donor to communicate with us at will—either with His or ours! Through our conscience, we strive to emulate the moral values of our donor.

Another of our Donor qualities is *spirit*! Spirit is not only the force by which we were able to breathe and act in this new environment of time, space, and matter. Spirit is also our means of staying in tune and in harmony with our Donor. Our Donor communicates with us through His Spirit—His essence of being!

That communication process is at its best when our conscience and spirit are operating in harmony. Consciousness allows us to monitor the relationship between our conscience and our spirit.

There is one other Donor quality that is linked to my consciousness. It is called *memory*! With memory, I am able to connect my thoughts, feelings, decisions, and actions with the various experiences that I may have.

Memory also connects my conscience and those same thoughts, feelings, decisions, and actions with the various experiences I may have! There in my memory, all of my thoughts, feelings, decisions, and actions are compared to my awareness of my Donor's expectations of me. And I am compelled to judge myself in light of the will and directives of my Donor. Here we are, Host-oriented creatures with Donor-oriented qualities!

There are, and were, no other creatures in all of our Donor's created order like us! We are souls!

> And God said, Let us make man in our image, after our likeness … So God created man in his own image, in the image of God created he him; male and female created he them. (Genesis 1:26a, 27)

Overcoming My Constraints

How much room, or space, does a soul need in which to exist and express itself? Almost immediately, I became conscious of my earthly constraints. And yet, as expansive as my Donor qualities are, I am experiencing the ability to manifest those Donor qualities in increments as my Host elements develop.

Within those constraints of time, the elements of fleshly matter begin to develop and expand. And with each phase of development and growth, the Host space to which I arrived began to enlarge.

I am also becoming more conscious about myself. I have developed a heart, lungs, legs, feet, arms, and hands, and I have also developed a brain, eyes, ears, a mouth, and a nose. I have a body in which so many other organs are developing. I can move. I can turn my developing body. I can kick. I can feel. I can feel warmth. I can feel cold. I can feel hunger. I can feel discomfort. I can feel pain. I can express my feelings.

The more I seek to express myself, the more I grow. The more I grow, the more conscious I become about myself and the effects of my growth on my Host. I am conscious of my Host. I learn more and more about her as each moment of time continues.

Every day my Host begins to emit various signals that indicate her consciousness about me!

She talks to me. She talks about how big I am becoming. She talks about how heavy I am getting. She even sings to me.

I am also becoming conscious of things happening beyond me and my Host. I hear conversations between my Host and someone who seems close to her. I hear other sounds that are becoming familiar. I am conscious of what is called day and night. I am conscious of what my Host calls peace and quiet. My body is growing. My constraints are diminishing. My consciousness is increasing.

I am taking on more and more of the characteristics of my Host. But even so, I am becoming more and more conscious of my Donor's presence. Even in this confined space, there is still room for me and my Donor.

Even under these constraints, inside this womb of limitations, I am conscious of—I feel the presence of—both my Donor and my Host. I am in her, but I also feel her inside me. I am taking on some of her qualities. I am in her, but I also feel my Donor inside me. I have not lost the qualities of my Donor. I am inside my Host, and yet I feel my Host and Donor inside me! Perhaps this is the way I will be able to accomplish my mission! I am a soul!

> And Adam knew Eve his wife; and she conceived, and bare Cain, and said, I have gotten a man from the Lord. (Genesis 4:1)

Who's There?

I can't see who it is, but somehow, I sense that I am not alone. Yes, I am already conscious of the presence of my Donor, but this "presence" is different! It is the presence of someone else—someone like me! Someone different from me but like me!

There is something else strange about this presence. Not only do I sense this other presence, and not only do I sense the presence of my Donor, but I also sense the presence of my donor *with* this other presence!

We can't talk to each other. We can't see each other. But I realize that we are both aware—we are both conscious—of each other. Both of us are growing in this same space. Not only am I becoming more conscious about myself, I am also becoming more conscious of this other presence.

It's interesting. We are two separate souls, yet we are in the same womb. We are two separate souls, yet we both possess the presence of my Donor. But something is different. We have the same Donor. We have the same Host. But we are two separate souls. I wonder if we have the same mission. If we don't, then what is the relationship between my mission and the mission of this soul beside me?

Maybe our "missions" are different! Seems like every time I turn inside my Host, that other soul seems to resist my moves. For some reason, I find myself doing the same thing when he moves. We're not pushing and shoving - there's not much room—but there is an ongoing "struggle" between us. For some reason I can feel a portion of his body. It seems to be at the end of one part of his body. We are so much alike, yet we are so much different.

How strange! Two different *souls* from the same Donor in the same Host on two different missions! And I still don't know who he is!

Maybe we are on two different missions. What will we be like when we see each other? If we are struggling inside of our Host, what will we be like when we begin to fulfill the missions that our Donor has given us?

> And the children struggled together within her; And she said, If it be so, why am I thus? And she went to enquire of the LORD. And the LORD said unto her, Two nations are in thy womb, and two manner of people shall be separated from thy bowels; and the one people shall be stronger than the other people, and the elder shall serve the younger.
> (Genesis 25:22–23)

The Great Escape

~

For the past several weeks, I have heard my Host talk about *time*. She speaks as if something is about to happen. She speaks as if my period of constraints is coming to a close. She speaks as if she and I will be able to experience a closer relationship. During this period of "time", my fleshly components have not only grown, but the space into which I arrived has grown also. And my consciousness has grown. My conscience is letting me know that the fulfillment of my mission cannot be accomplished in this current space. I must escape this realm of constraints!

Then it happened! That enclosure in which I had been developing began to undergo great turmoil. That enclosure, that womb, began to undergo a series of contractions. I was being squeezed one moment and being relieved the next. Before long that watery substance began to diminish. I thought those constraints were uncomfortable enough before, but now they had become unbearable. My Host was in pain, and so was I. We both began to fight—she for me and herself and I for her and myself! We fought together!

In those constraining moments, my conscience would not let me surrender to the constraints being imposed on me. I was on a mission, and whatever constraints I was under, I was compelled to fulfill my mission—for my Host's sake, and for my Donor's sake!

She cried in pain, and I struggled in pain. And then, I found an opening! I struggled to escape those constraints under which I had been living. I struggled to get free. With one final contraction by my Host, *I escaped!*

Her crying stopped, and mine began. I cried out in relief! I cried out in joy! I was conscious of a sense of freedom! I was no longer under those constraints of my Host's womb! I became conscious of others in our presence. I was now living under new circumstances. I could move my arms and legs without resistance. I could open my eyes and actually see other objects and people. I could hear new sounds. I could smell new and different fragrances and odors. I could feel the difference between various things.

My Host was still there! And I was also conscious of the presence of my Donor. A sense of peace overcame me. My mission had not been aborted. Soon I was fast asleep.

> Unto the woman he said, I will greatly multiply thy sorrow, and thy conception; in sorrow thou shalt bring forth children ... (Genesis 3:16a)

Know Thyself

When I'm not sleeping, I have discovered something exciting and interesting. I can distinguish the presence and differences of various things around me. I have been looking around at my surroundings. I can *see!* Every day my eyes begin to focus on various objects around me. I have also been observing my Host, and I am learning about another being, who also gives me much attention. He seems to have a familiar attachment to me and to my Host that resembles the attachment she has for me.

While I am looking and seeing various things around me, I am also becoming able to understand the connection between some of the things that I see, with various things that I also hear! That's right! I also hear different sounds around me. Some are pleasant, and some are disturbing! The disturbing ones upset me, and I begin to respond with sounds of my own. I cry! And when I cry, I have also discovered that my Host, and sometimes her companion, will pick me up and cradle me close to them.

Together they have been attending to several feelings and actions that seem to emanate from my body. I am becoming more and more aware of my body. But my Host is the primary one who cradles me close to herself and presses a small portion of her body to my mouth. A warm substance oozes into my mouth, especially as I make sucking actions.

In those moments, I sense a connection with my Host that resembles the connection I have with my Donor. Maybe that sense of connection also explains my efforts to respond to these different feelings.

For some reason, I not only cry out in moments of discomfort, but I also find myself trying to make similar sounds that I hear my Host and her companion and others making with their mouths. Soon I'm going to talk just like them!

I also find my consciousness of my "self" increasing. More and more I am learning to use each component of my body. I have discovered that I have two appendages at the top and at the bottom of my body. Those two top appendages at the end of arms allow me to grasp and feel things, and I can use them try to draw things to my mouth. I can even grasp those two bottom appendages at the end of my legs! It's a little harder to draw them to my mouth, but I'm getting better at that effort.

Not only am I becoming better able to see, hear, feel, and speak, but as the weeks and months have gone by, I am also becoming able to stand up on my feet! I knew they had a better purpose than just putting them into my mouth.

I am understanding that my consciousness allows me to maintain a constant connection with myself, with my Host, and with my Donor. I am learning that the mind of my Donor helps me understand the actions of my Host.

She keeps repeating certain words like, "I love you," and when she does, I become conscious of her spirit reaching out to my spirit. And in those moments, I become even more conscious of the presence of my Donor. What she calls "love" resembles a feeling similar to that which I experienced in the presence of my Donor before my initial departure.

It must be! At some point in time, my Host must have also experienced the presence of my Donor! That sense of His presence endears me to fulfill my mission. Could it be that each of these characteristics is intended to enable me to accomplish the mission, which my Donor assigned for me?

But most of all, I can think! My consciousness reveals my ability to make logical, systematic, and emotional connections between the things I see, hear, feel, and taste. The ability and process of making those logical and systematic connections with all the things that I experience and remember is thought in operation.

I am a Soul! *A Living Soul!*

∽

> I will praise thee;
> for I am fearfully and wonderfully made: marvelous
> are thy works; and that my soul knoweth right well.
> (Psalm 139:14)

Feeding Time

My consciousness of myself continues to increase. At first certain feelings would arise within me that made me conscious of a sense of need. Something within me seemed to be craving something beyond me. I noticed that when those moments came upon me, I would begin to cry out—sometimes softly, sometimes with great declaration! And when I did, seemingly without hesitation, my Host would press that small portion of her body to my mouth.

As that warm substance oozed into my mouth, I found myself experiencing a sense of not only great satisfaction, but also great fulfillment! I soon began to seek frequent encounters with my Host when those feelings came.

Those feelings were so intense that I would begin to cry out, and when I did, seemingly without hesitation, my Host would cuddle me in her arms and press that small portion of her body to my mouth again. I soon came to understand the deeper meaning of the word *breast*. Somehow, the last portion of the sound of that word had deeper meaning—"rest"!

As the hart panteth after the water brooks, so panteth my soul after thee, O God.
My soul thirsteth for God, for the Living God ...
(Psalm 42:1, 2a)

Learning to Walk

My consciousness of the things I desire makes me also conscious of the things that I seek and the extent to which I strive to access them. My will lets me decide what I want for myself! I have also discovered that I have the ability to access some of those things. I am beginning to stand and move from one place to another—on my own!

I can walk! My steps are not always steady, but I am learning to hold on to things, and to people, as I go from place to place. Sometimes I can go quite far before I fall or just sit down. But I am walking! I have personal access to this world in which I live.

The more I walk—the more I move from where I was—the larger my world becomes! Sometimes as I walk from place to place, I forget about my Host and all the other *souls* that I've come to know. That is, until I reach a place where I can't go any farther, or realize that I am in an unfamiliar setting, or that I need others to help me reach my intended destination.

Walking is good, but I am beginning to realize that walking is more exciting and fulfilling when I have a destination to reach. Sometimes

I find myself wanting to walk, but certain situations that I am facing hinder me.

∾

> What doth the LORD require of thee, but to … walk humbly with thy God? (Micah 6:8)

Independence Day

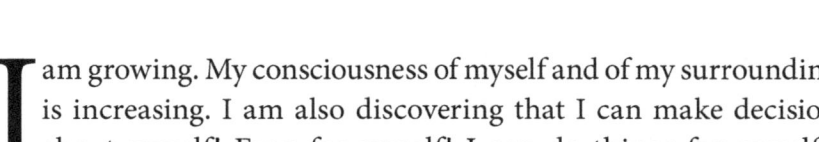

I am growing. My consciousness of myself and of my surroundings is increasing. I am also discovering that I can make decisions about myself! Even for myself! I can do things for myself. I can do some things on my own, by myself. I am feeling a sense of "independence"! —Freedom! I can decide to do what I want to do. I can even decide what I want to think about!

Uh-oh! I just began to realize that some of the things I think about are creating a problem in my consciousness. Some of the things I think about directly conflict with some of the instructions of my Host. Some of the things I think about directly conflict with the moral values of my Donor!

The more I hear those words, "No, no!" and "Stop!" the more I sense an inner struggle. There is a conflict between what I want to think and do with what my conscience reminds me about my Donor. There are things that I don't want to think and do that my conscience reminds me that my Donor wants me to do. I am free, but I am not truly independent!

I am still a soul. I am still a Holy Being! I am still directly connected to my Donor! I cannot really function apart from my Donor. Somehow I must learn to balance what I want with what my Donor wants for me.

∽

> Nevertheless, not as I will, but as thou wilt.
> (Matthew 26:39)

The Inner Struggle

I am growing. The more I grow, the more I am conscious of a great struggle taking place within me. Something seems to draw me away from my Donor's Will for me and from my Mission! Something seems to cause me to seek personal pleasure in the things that impact my body. The more I focus on my body, the less I focus on my Donor's Will for me and on my Mission!

The other day I heard something about the First Host and her Companion. I understand that they were also the First **Souls** that my Donor had created I understand that they were also given a Mission to accomplish, but that both of them became so enamored with things that might satisfy their bodies and their minds that they disobeyed the Donor! And when they disobeyed the Donor, they were destined to suffer the consequences!

Their relationship with the Donor was changed! Their nature was changed! No longer were they spiritual creatures in flesh! Now they had become carnal creatures with a fleshly focus, yet still having a spiritual conscience, consciousness, *and* mission! And all of the souls which came from them were born in that Fallen State, that self-focused state, having a sinful nature!

The more I thought about what I had heard, the more I realized that that is what I was experiencing. I was experiencing the consequences of the "Fall" – a Sin Nature!

Realizing what is happening within me, I am constantly challenged to consciously choose between the desires of my flesh and the directives of my mission.

From time to time, I find myself struggling with the conflicts between my spirit and my flesh. Many times my fleshly desires not only conflict with my spiritual desires, but they also hinder the fulfillment of my mission.

Another soul later expressed that sin nature in this manner:

> For the good that I would I do not: but the evil which I would not I do.
> (Romans 7:19)

Getting the Help I Need

I am growing. My consciousness of myself and my surroundings is increasing. I am becoming able to do more and more things on my own each day.

During my interactions with my Host and others around me, I am discovering that my inner struggles are similar to those I encounter. Right and wrong, urges and temptations, principles and values—the experiences increase every day.

In the midst of all of these experiences, I am also feeling the presence of my Donor's Spirit! Something about His presence energizes my spirit. Something about His presence also enables my mind to think and understand things I had not envisioned before. Something about His presence also enables my body to do things I had never done before. Something about His presence also stimulates my conscience.

The more I grow and the more I know, the more I begin to realize another problem—keeping the things that I am learning in harmony with my Donor's Will and Mission for me!

I am discovering that, the more I allow my spirit to follow my Donor's Spirit, the better I am able to avoid many problems in my relationships with my Host, with those whom I encounter and interact with, and with my Donor.

∾

> And Jesus increased in wisdom and stature, and in favour with God and man. (Luke 2:52)

Section 2
SOUL MEN AND SOUL WOMEN

A Special Gift

―――――― ∾ ――――――

I understand that every soul, like me, is a gift of my Donor to those whom He has seen fit to entrust its development and nurture. But I also understand that some souls are special gifts! I am one of them.

My Host was not like most mothers. For many years, she wanted to be a Host, but she was not so blessed. Year after year, sadness and sorrow became her daily companions. Even the loving encouragement of her husband was not enough to lessen her anguish.

Then one day she took her burden to my Donor. At the Temple in Shiloh, she made a special vow – if my Donor would give her a son, she would give him back to Him for as long as he lived. The priest of the temple confirmed her promise and encouraged her in her faith in my Donor.

Not too long after, my Donor answered her prayers. He blessed her with *me*! She became my Host, and I became her answered prayer—her Special Gift!

I soon came to understand something else special about myself. My Host, who had prayed so hard and long to become a Host, had also chosen to give me back to my Donor! I, who had become a special gift of my Donor to my Host, now have become the Special Gift of my Host to my Donor!

From an early age, my Host entrusted me to the Priest—another special servant.

His assignment was to render special service in leading other souls to worship our Donor!

It was not long before I came to realize that I also had a special relationship with my Donor.

No longer was I growing up in the house of my Host. Instead, I was growing up in the House of my Donor—I was growing up in the House of the Lord!

> For this child I prayed; and the LORD hath given me my petition which I asked of him. Therefore also I have lent him to the LORD; As long as he liveth, he shall be lent to the LORD. (1 Samuel 1:27–28)

Challenges to Service

The more I grow, the more I learn about my relationship with my Donor and His relationship with the other souls I encounter each day. The more I render my service in the House of my Donor, the closer I seem to draw to my Donor.

I see other souls come every day to strengthen their relationships with my Donor. Yet I also see the fellow servants of my Donor doing things that dishonor my Donor. If we are serving the same Donor, then why is their "service" so different, so disrespectful, from mine? Why are they doing things that cause confusion of and abuse to those whom we serve? Why do they rebel against the Will of our Donor?

Why do they steal and desecrate the sacrifices of those coming to strengthen their relationships with our Donor? Why do they mislead the women worshipers and cause them to sin *in* the House of our Donor?

What can I do? They know what they are doing. They have been serving much longer than I have. Why doesn't our leader do something to stop them? How can I stop such actions? I am so much younger than they are! Why is their service so much different from mine? Why is their behavior so much different from mine? Their behavior causes me to wonder about their relationship with our Donor.

∾

> Now the sons of Eli were sons of Belial: they knew not the LORD. (1 Samuel 2:12)

Listening to the Right Voice

I have been serving my Donor. I have been doing what I have been told to do. I have been given a very special task to perform in the House of my Donor—I help to keep the Lamp of my Donor lit at all times.

That Lamp symbolizes the Presence of our Donor. If it ever goes out, it might cause great fear and dread among the other souls in our community. I have learned the sense of security and hope that the Lamp brings.

Every time I pour in more oil, I can sense the Presence of my Donor. I feel Him near, yet I have never spoken to Him, nor have I ever heard Him speak to me. I know the voice of Eli. I know the voices of his sons, Hophni and Phinehas. I know the voices of many of those who come to worship our Donor here at His House. But I have never heard the Voice of our Donor! I have seen many of the faces of those whose voices I have heard. But I have never even seen nor heard our Donor!

One night it happened! One night I heard His Voice! I was sleeping, and my Donor spoke to me! At first, I did not know who was calling my name. I thought it might have been Eli. I rushed up from my bed and ran to Eli. He sought to comfort me, assuring me that it was not him calling me.

Three times, I heard His Voice! Three times, I ran to Eli! Blind though he was, Eli began to see what was happening to me. Eli had been serving our Donor long enough to know that when our Donor has something special for His servants to do, He would personally speak to them! So, he told me what to do.

The next time I heard my Donor call me, I responded as Eli had instructed. I acknowledged not only the Presence of my Donor, but also His Voice! And from that moment on, I learned not only to serve my Donor, but I also learned to listen to and obey the Voice of my Donor!

> And Samuel grew, and the LORD was with him, and did let none of his words fall to the ground.
> (1 Samuel 3:19)

Close Encounters

I am still growing. My consciousness of myself, and of my Host, is increasing. I have been in confinement for about six months now. Within the past month, a few visitors have come by to visit with my Host. I can make out certain expressions of seeming concern about my Host's condition, especially in her old age. No one seemed to have known that I had become a part of her life.

Yesterday, my Host had another visitor. This visit was quite different from the others. I can sense the presence of my Host's companion. But yesterday, I became aware of the presence of some other beings! I heard expressions of salutations being exchanged between my Host and one of them. I also heard my Host identify her as "the mother of my Lord"!

Maybe that explains why I found myself being filled with exuberance also at that moment. For some reason I also felt the Presence of my Donor! The sense of His Presence was so great that I found myself literally leaping in that confined space that they called a womb! Apparently I was not the only one to sense that awesome Presence! Something about that awesome Presence seemed to have infused the total being of my Host! She began expressing words of awe and praise at the presence of her visitor.

And then her visitor began singing a song that I had not heard before. It was a song about my Donor! She sang about various deeds that my Donor either had done or was about to do, seemingly in reference to that awesome Presence that I also was quite conscious of when she first came into our presence. For almost three months, we shared a close proximity, and then He was gone.

It was some thirty years later before our paths met again! This time, there were no physical constraints. This time I saw—I came face-to-face with—the One whose presence first caused me to leap with joy! But this time our encounter was different!

I was busy following my mission from my Donor—proclaiming the Coming of the Messiah! My message called sinners to repent of their sins and to publicly affirm their change of spiritual direction through the act of baptism.

While I was baptizing some repentant souls, He came into my presence once more! This time He presented Himself as one who needed baptism! Recognizing who He was and realizing what He had come to do, I humbly sought *Him* to baptize *me*! Upon His gracious refusal and admonition for me to fulfill my mission from my Donor, I complied with His request and baptized Him!

One of the most memorable experiences of that moment was when the Presence of my Donor was manifested by *His* Spirit. And my Donor's Voice was heard by all around! "This is my beloved Son, in whom I am well pleased," He said!

Something about obeying the Will of my Donor makes His Presence last for Eternity!

And the child grew, and waxed strong in spirit, and was in the desert till the day of his showing unto Israel.
(Luke 1:80)

In My Right Mind

Some said I had lost my mind. Others said I was crazy. Others said I was full of the devil. I don't know what happened to me, but at a point in time—I don't remember when—my behavior changed. My relationships with people changed. I became violent! I became belligerent! I became strong—much stronger than many men put together. No one was able to subdue me. I could even break chains!

I don't know what happened. I do recall having friends. I do recall having people talk to me, interacting with me. But because of my behavior, people stayed away from me. I was lonely. I became a homeless vagrant. I was hurt and I was hurting, and I became a "hurter". People had problems with me, and I had problems with myself. I took my anger and agony and pain out on myself. I became self-abusive, even cutting my body with stones!

I was like a living dead man. Perhaps that's why I made the graveyard my dwelling place. It seems like I was either talking to some spirits, or they were talking to me. Everywhere I turned, evil thoughts, evil ideas, evil feelings were all around me – even *in* me! Those evil spirits – those demons—had taken control of me! My thoughts were their thoughts, and their thoughts were always against me! I was conscious of myself, but I had little control over myself. They had control over my body and my mind.

But one day it happened. I felt the presence of another Spirit! I looked around, and there He was!

He looked no different from any other person I had seen and interacted with before, but He *was* different! Something about Him spoke to something deep down inside me.

Even in my deranged mental state and my disheveled physical state, something about Him communicated with something inside *me*! Even though those demons had control over my body and my mind, they did not have control over my spirit!

When I saw Him, I sensed the presence of my Donor! And when I sensed the presence of my Donor, something about His Presence affirmed to me my purpose! Something about His Spirit revived my spirit!

Even the presence and power of five thousand demons could not overcome my desire to draw close to Him. I immediately left where I was and ran to where He was! In that moment I recognized His spiritual relationship to my Donor—He was the Son of my Donor! I even called Him by name—Jesus!

Now, in that moment of union between my spirit and His Spirit, those five thousand evil spirits dwelling and operating within me became extremely uncomfortable. They who had been tormenting me now felt the overpowering presence of Jesus! And since evil cannot dwell in the presence of holiness, and since my spirit had found spiritual harmony with His Spirit, those evil spirits knew they had to find a new dwelling place.

So "Legion", as they called themselves, appealed to the Lord for new lodging. They left me, and I found Him. And when I found Him, I found my true self. I found my spiritual self!

All of those demonic thoughts and feelings and actions were gone. They no longer controlled my spirit! They no longer controlled my body! They no longer controlled my mind! My mind was from then on in harmony with the Mind of my Donor.

Whatever my past has been, my future, my body, my spirit, and my mind shall be focused on the mission that my Donor gave me when I embarked on this Earth. My mind is made up. My soul is at peace!

∽

> And they come to Jesus, and see him that had the legion, sitting, and clothed, and in his right mind ... (Mark 5:15)

A Second Chance to Live

------ ◠◡ ------

Death may be welcomed by some elderly souls. But when you are young, death is not welcomed! There are things to do, places to go, and people to see.

I had seen others in our family and in our community die, mostly old folk. But I was young, only twelve years old, in human years. My life was before me. Yet something was happening within me. Whatever explanations anyone had were hard to understand. Simply stated, I was *dying*!

Dying! Death! Dead! They are terms that bring great fear to many, anguish to some, a sense of hopelessness to others, and sorrow to most. Now they said it was happening to me! And it was nothing that I, or anyone else, could do about it! Even the physicians in the community had made that same prognosis.

But my father had not given up hope! He left my deathbed and went looking for a man—a man who had helped others in my situation.

While he was gone, I was conscious of the various things that were going on around me. I was conscious of my Host—my mother—trying to comfort me. I was conscious of others in the room—some crying, some quoting passages of scripture, and others praying.

Many thoughts and questions were going through my mind. What really is death? What really happens in the body when death happens? What really happens to the memory when death happens? Will it hurt?

I remember hearing their voices. And then, I lost my consciousness!

Whatever happened from that moment on, I have no idea. I can't even remember when it happened. I simply lost consciousness!

When I lost consciousness, apparently, I must have also stopped breathing, and those around me came to the conclusion that I had died! After all, I had stopped breathing.

And when I stopped breathing, I could no longer control the animation of my body. Something about death includes the cessation of breathing, the end of bodily functions, and the loss of consciousness.

But this loss of consciousness was much different and deeper than any sleep I had ever experienced. I had fallen asleep many times before, but after my sleep I always returned to the same status of life. Often I would be awakened by a voice—my mother's or my father's. But this time was different. This time I heard another voice. But it was not my mother's, or my father's, or any other voice that I could recall. This was a very special *voice*!

When I heard it, something about that voice revived my consciousness! But something about that voice also made me conscious of the presence of someone else—a special Presence! It was as if my Donor was present with me! I heard a voice, and I felt my Donor's Presence!

I also felt the hand of the One who spoke—He was holding my hand. Something about His touch, something about my hand in His gave me new strength. Then that voice simply said, *"Maid, arise."* In that instant, I began breathing again. In obedience to His voice, and animated with renewed strength in my body, I got up!

Empowered with a renewed spirit, I got up—and ate food—like a twelve-year-old girl likes to do!

I can't explain what all had happened, nor could my parents. But the man behind that voice simply told all of us not to tell anyone what had been done.

After all of the neighbors had gone home and things started getting back to normal, I began to focus more on my purpose and plans for the future. Something about the memory of that voice and the reassuring tone of those words, *"Maid, arise,"* caused me to realize that I had been given a second chance to live.

Somehow, in spite of my father being active in the synagogue, my focus on religion and God had not been strong. I'm sure I'm not the only one. But after what has happened, I am more conscious and desirous of a closer relationship with God.

Those words, *"Arise! Arise! Arise!"* keep coming back to me. There must be something special about me. There must be something special that God wants me to do. I am on a mission! My life has divine purpose! I am no longer dead! I am alive!

I am once again a Living Soul!

> The hour is coming, and now is, when the dead shall hear the voice of the Son of God: and they that hear shall live. (John 5:25)

Section 3
RECOMPENSE

Mission Aborted

It seemed as if all systems were a go. My development was progressing as designed by my Donor. Not only were my sensory systems developing, but I could also hear as well as feel. I was conscious of uncomfortable stimuli around me.

Suddenly I began to sense tension and turmoil in my Host. It seemed as if my development began to present problems to my Host. I could not fully understand the source of those feelings. One moment I could sense anger in my Host. At some moments, I would sense fear. At certain other moments, there was the feeling of opposition to my presence.

I could not understand what was happening. I was developing properly, as planned by my Donor, but my development seemed to create problems for my Host. She began to express a desire to bring those problems to an end.

I began hearing the term *abortion* in her conversations. More and more that term began to be expressed. Various possible options and consequences were discussed. Some options would allow my Host to continue on with some of her previous plans for life—without me.

To my Host, that term and the options seemed to bring a sense of relief. But, the more I heard it, the more I became concerned. Somehow, that term and those options seemed to indicate a cessation of my mission! Somehow, I began to feel turmoil within myself.

"Abortion"—cessation of my Host's fears, and anxieties! "Abortion"—cessation of my Donor's feelings, will, and concerns!

"Abortion"—cessation of my Life! "Abortion"—cessation of my mission!

While my Host focused on ending her anxieties, she seemed to have little or no concern about *me*! However my Donor felt, and whatever He had intended for *me*, if my Host did what she was thinking and feeling, *my* life could be ended! My mission was in jeopardy!

Not long after that my Host made her decision. Abortion it was!

I didn't know what to expect next. But I could feel my Host lying down. The planned procedures had been discussed. My Host would be sedated. She would be "put to sleep." And then some type of substance would be injected into me. She would not feel anything—but I would!

After a short period of time, I would experience much pain and eventual death! Then the doctor would pull and/or scrape my body parts from within my Host's womb! And I—all of my body parts—would be discarded like other forms of trash! There could be no worse form of home eviction than that!

No one sought my opinion. No one knew or seemed to care about my mission. The decision had been made, and the process was underway. Suddenly I began to experience great discomfort and then extreme pain! And … then I lost consciousness!

My Host later awoke and soon went home—without me! I was dead!

Whatever my Donor had in store for me to do for Him had been aborted! Whatever my Donor had in store for me to do for others in this world—My mission—had been aborted!

In the eyes of some, I was dead. For some others, I never was. But in the mind of my Donor, though unconscious, I am still a Living Soul!

> He hath also prepared for him the instruments of death ... (Psalm 7:13)

Destined for Damnation

———————— ∽ ————————

Unlike those with whom I traveled and partnered—although many of our experiences were the same—my destiny was different. I too had personally encountered the Son of my Donor. He specifically chose me, along with the others, for a special mission!

In preparation for that mission, we spent three years in training, disciplining, and spiritual nurturing. During our training period, He revealed to us the deeper truths of the scriptures. He instilled in us a sense of compassion that transcended the teachings and practices of the scribes and Pharisees who taught the rest of our people. On many occasions, we watched Him teach in the synagogues and in the Temple. We were witnesses to His mastery of the Word of our Donor. In His presence, we felt the power and presence of our Donor.

We—even I—were empowered by Him to heal the sick, give sight to the blind, cast out demons, and even raise the dead! He gave me a special role among the others—I was responsible for the fiscal resources of the group.

Not much has been written about me, but that which is written sets the stage for my destiny. Like all the others, I knew the Jewish leaders sought to kill Jesus. He had told us that on several occasions. I am the one who betrayed Jesus! I am the one who personally approached the chief Priests and volunteered to betray Jesus to them.

Somehow my Donor's ultimate purpose for me got overshadowed by my personal hopes and anticipations. Whether I became dissatisfied with Jesus' increasing references to His impending death; whether I wanted to force a confrontation between Him and the Jewish rulers; or whether I had ulterior motives for myself is not the issue in my betraying Jesus.

The real issue is that, whatever was happening around me, I chose to put my aspirations above my Donor's mission for me.

Keep in mind, the purpose for my Donor's Son was to save *all* souls from the penalty of sin and to reconcile all souls to a holy relationship to our Donor. For that cause, the Son of our Donor specifically chose and included *me* in helping to accomplish those divine goals.

It's not important to try to explain why I went to the chief priests and offered to betray Jesus. I'm not quite sure how I could rationalize, let alone justify, my actions. Somehow, I came to realize that to kiss someone in a false act of a traitor's love soon loses whatever value or benefit that may have been intended. I didn't ask for it, and although I took it, I realized that I had done more damage than those thirty pieces of silver could ever repay. I couldn't keep it. I returned it to those who gave it to me. But the damage had already been done.

I had chosen to place *my* will over that of my Donor and of His Son. That choice in itself was an act of sin!

But the nature of my sin was all the more heinous in that I also sought to change the will of my Donor and the purpose of sending His Son into this world. This was an act of evil! That must be why Jesus called me "the son of perdition"! My decision to betray Jesus into the hands of His enemies was an act of evil!

Evil is the work of the Evil One—Satan! Right there, in that upper room—right there, after He had explained the relationship between the Unleavened Bread and His Body, and the Fruit of the Vine and His Blood it was *then* that my true nature was revealed! I had committed myself to the will of Satan! I determined in my heart to *betray* Jesus! Instead of remaining true to my Donor's mission for me, I chose to accept the mission of the Evil One.

Jesus had previously told us all, before I left to betray Him, that He was leaving soon to prepare a special place for each of us in Heaven. For whatever reason, I was focusing more on my plans for Him on Earth, rather than His plans for all of His Disciples and Believers in Heaven.

In spite of my public, social, and religious relationship with Jesus, I failed to accept God's purpose and plan for Jesus! And when I rejected God's purpose and plan for Jesus on Earth, I also rejected God's purpose and plan for *ME* in Heaven!

Unlike that lost son that He spoke about in one of His parables, when I came to myself, I regretted what I had done, but that regret focused on *me*!

I regretted, but I never repented! I was sorry for what I had done, but I never repented *of* what I had done! I never turned away from following the Evil One!

His purpose on Earth was to "kill, steal, and destroy" every soul that he could, especially those souls that sought to obey the directives of the Donor! The Evil One had used *me* to kill the Son of God!

Then he used my guilt and remorse from my evil deed against myself! I was so sorry *for* myself that I could not live *with myself* on Earth! Nor was I worthy to live with God in Heaven!

But my greater sin was that I also chose not to accept the greater part of God's plan of salvation through Jesus Christ. I made one of the biggest mistakes that any soul could ever make. I had sinned, but I forfeited, I failed to accept, God's forgiveness of my sins.

I had one more evil thought—I chose to kill myself! No wonder Jesus called me the "son of perdition". Perdition—destruction—is my destiny! In all that I have done, I am still a soul—a Lost Soul!

> My Eternal Future, my Eternal Destiny, is Hell!

> But woe unto that man by whom the Son of man is betrayed! it had been good for that man if he had not been born. (Matthew 26:24)

An Intermission

Forgive me for not being able to share the details of this portion of my adventure. I am experiencing an intermission in my soul's adventure. I believe it is what is called death! It is an experience, I understand, that all souls must experience at some phase in their existence.

One moment I was conscious—aware of my environment, my thoughts, my past, my plans for my future. Then I lost consciousness. At points in time, I could remember, but this time my memory is not in operation. It is not like when I had fallen asleep. Even in my sleep, I could exercise memory and thinking—that's what happened in my dreams. But now I am not aware of time, pain, location, or what else is happening around me. This experience is unlike any I have ever had. I am more than unconscious! I am dead!

I understood that other souls would also be in this state of existence. If they are, we cannot communicate. I am not aware of what has happened to me or what was happening to them in this state. We all must be unconscious!

Yet there was the expectation, even assurance, that this phase of my existence was not permanent. Whatever was happening, whatever was going on, this experience was only an intermission of my conscious existence. I am a soul in the state of death! Something better or worse is yet to follow!

∽

> And as it is appointed unto men once to die, but after this the judgment ... (Hebrews 9:27)

Souls on Trial

I have no idea how long my period of unconsciousness lasted. All of a sudden I was conscious—alive—again. This time I was not alone.

I had been in crowds before—theaters and churches and stadiums—but this time this crowd was incomprehensible. There were more souls than I have ever encountered. And we all were standing together, before our Donor! From some I sensed awe and from others a sense of dread.

Then some Great Books were opened. From them, each of our names and the deeds we had done while on our respective assignments from our Donor were read. The countenance of many of those standing around me suddenly changed—after their respective names were called and their deeds revealed. Some expressed guilt and sorrow. Others expressed satisfaction and joy.

From these books, the deeds of each of those souls were revealed, and judgment was made whether they complied with the directives of our Donor.

And then another Book was opened. It was called the Book of Life. Once again, names were called. But this time, many names that had been called out of the previous books were omitted!

Then those souls whose names had not been written in the Book of Life were cast into a great Lake of Fire! These were the souls that had failed to obey the directives of our Donor. These were they whose eternal destiny was with the Adversary of our Donor—Satan and his fallen angels.

During my adventures on Earth, I heard the moans and cries of agony and sorrow and pain from many souls. But when those souls were cast into that great Lake of Fire, when they joined Satan and his fallen angels, there were cries of agony and woe like I have never heard before!

Interestingly, those cries of agony didn't seem to be caused by that great Lake of Fire! Instead, the moans and expressions of agony seemed to reflect sounds of guilt and despair because of something else that they had begun to experience. Those cries were about the indescribable anguish of experiencing the separation of their Souls from the presence of Almighty God! With or without those flames, those indescribable cries of anguish were enough for me to realize that having my soul separated from the presence of God is really what makes hell *HELL*!

Some of those cries were from souls I knew. Some of those cries were from souls who had the same Hosts, and some were from the same families. For them, that had to be the saddest family reunion ever!

But when I heard *my* name being called from that Book of Life, a sense of joy welled up within me! I knew that I had done some of the same things that those hell-destined souls had done. I knew that I had done some worse things than many of them had done. But there was one deed written in that Book of Life that I had done that they had failed to do.

I confessed and repented of my sinful deeds! I sought the forgiveness of my Donor for those sinful deeds. I accepted His saving substitute for my transgressions against Him—Jesus the Christ!

I entrusted the rest of my life and my heavenly mission to the guidance and empowerment of His Holy Spirit. And because of those decisions that I made about my mission from my Donor, my name was included in that Book of Life!

I would share the rest of my adventure with you, but your real joy and appreciation for my adventure will come when you fulfill the Donor's mission for your soul.

> Come, ye blessed of my Father, inherit the kingdom prepared for you from the foundation of the world ... (Matthew 25:34)

Because of Me

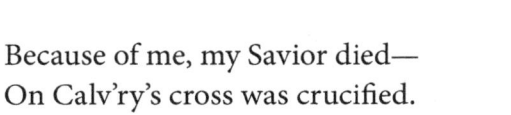

Because of me, my Savior died—
On Calv'ry's cross was crucified.
The price of sin for me was paid—
By His own blood my death was stayed.

    Because of me, Creation cried—
    The sun behind the clouds did hide.
    The morning stars in sorrow sang—
    The Earth replied in solemn strain.

Because of me, in Joseph's tomb,
My Lord was laid to change my doom.
In darkness all alone He stayed—
My ransomed price of death was paid.

    Chorus 1
    O praise His name, who, free from guile,
    Forgave my sins—made me His child;
    Redeemed my soul and set me free,
    He did it all because of me!

Because of me—that Sunday morn
The Grave was burst—asunder torn;
The grip of Death was paralyzed.
To Eternal Shores my soul shall rise!

    Because of me, Christ shall return!
    His face mine eyes shall soon discern.
    Through cloven skies He shall descend
    And rapture me and you, my friend!

Because of me, dear Calv'ry's Lamb
Prepared a feast—a guest I am.
With saints, who have through fires been tried,
We'll all sit down—the Savior's bride!

    Chorus 2
    Praise Him, my soul, for I have found
    My name is also written down
    Inside His Book of Life, you see—
    He did it all because of me!

Samuel W. Hale, Jr.
©1985

Printed in the USA
CPSIA information can be obtained
at www.ICGtesting.com
JSHW020936050923
47703JS00006B/105